CRIPPLED

A PLAY BY

PAUL DAVID POWER

BREAKWATER
P.O. Box 2188, St. John's, NL, Canada, A1C 6E6
WWW.BREAKWATERBOOKS.COM

COPYRIGHT © 2021 Paul David Power
ISBN 978-1-55081-893-2

A CIP catalogue record for this book is available from Library and Archives Canada

Cover photograph: Chris Hibbs
Dramatic series editor: Robert Chafe

We acknowledge the support of the Canada Council for the Arts. We acknowledge the financial support of the Government of Canada through the Department of Heritage and the Government of Newfoundland and Labrador through the Department of Tourism, Culture, Arts and Recreation for our publishing activities.

PRINTED AND BOUND IN CANADA.

  Canada Council   Conseil des arts
for the Arts   du Canada

Canada

 Newfoundland Labrador

Breakwater Books is committed to choosing papers and materials for our books that help to protect our environment. To this end, this book is printed on recycled paper that is certified by the Forest Stewardship Council®.

FOR JONATHAN

INTRODUCTION

Grief is at once a barrier and a beacon. It prevents us from moving forward, becoming the only thing we can see in its overwhelming power. At the same time, it is a light in the tunnel, pulling us forward in the elusive search for our lost one: that perfect moment that proved they were here and alive; our need to see them again in the most simple and mundane of moments; those moments that ring with their individuality and their connection to us, all-encompassing and yet tiny and specific.

Sitting in the LSPU Hall the night that I first heard an early reading of *Crippled*, I was thunderstruck by the grief I felt for Paul and his loss and how it mirrored my own journey. I was compelled to offer, almost beg, to work on this show with him because somehow, he captured the heart of the grief I had experienced, and he had put into words what I, and so many others, could not. I wanted to honour that and be there for him. In a way it was kind of selfish, in the way that grief is both selfish and self-less; it is about us and about them.

Navigating that grief and trauma with love and joy under-pinned every part of the rehearsal process. We had a very loose structure that had us moving through each moment of the play in detail, yet at a pace that kept Paul's heart and mind at the forefront. As we went through this—day after day, month after month, year after year, on page and on stage, with each other and in front of others—respect for Paul was always at the forefront.

And, as painful as moments of this play are, it is the absolute magic of the love and joy that Paul has captured that has kept me following along. Somehow, in the very uniqueness of Paul and Jonathan's life and story, there is something that speaks to me and resonates so deeply that I just can't get enough of it. Based on the reactions of audiences everywhere, this play really does heal with joy.

I am so glad that Paul let me join his journey. May you enter this story with curiosity, and bravery, like Paul, and may it bring you the love and joy that we have all experienced in his capable hands.

Danielle Irvine
May 2021

CRIPPLED

Crippled was first produced by Power Productions at The Resource Centre for the Arts (LSPU Hall) in St. John's, NL in February 2018, with the following artistic team:

CAST:

Evan/Jonathan	*Pat Dempsey*
Tony/Paul	*Paul David Power*
Carl	*Matt White*

Directed by *Danielle Irvine*

Lighting Design and Video Production by *Robert Gauthier*

Sound Design by *George Robertson*

Set Design by *Kirsti Mikoda, Danielle Irvine*

Stage Management by *Kirsti Mikoda*

Assistant Stage Management by *Julie Brocklehurst, Janet O'Reilly, Kim White*

Dramaturgy by *Robert Chafe*

Audio Description by *Kat Germain*

ASL Interpretation by *Heather Crane, Dana Rideout*

NOTE: To maintain the integrity of the story, the role of TONY should be performed by an artist who self-identifies as living with a physical disability. Minor changes to text are permitted to reflect the specific physical disability of the artist portraying Tony.

St. John's waterfront at night.

In the centre of the dock stands TONY, *supported by crutches. He is fixated on the water—almost in a trance.*

After a few moments, TONY *brings his feet to the edge of the dock. It's not quite clear if he is just looking or planning to jump. He moves closer to the edge.*

EVAN *enters.*

EVAN: Hey! You okay?

TONY: *(startled)* What? Yeah...I'm fine.

EVAN: You gotta be careful down here. You never know when you might slip.

TONY: I'm good.

EVAN *moves closer.*

EVAN: You sure? It's pretty icy.

TONY: I'm sure. Thanks.

Awkward pause. EVAN *moves alongside* TONY, *who is still looking out over the water.*

EVAN: So, where you headed?

TONY: What?

EVAN: Headed. Where you headed?

TONY: Nowhere. I'm just hangin' out here.

EVAN: Pretty cold night to just be hangin' out on the waterfront.

TONY *looks at* EVAN *and then back at the water.*

TONY: It's pretty mild.

EVAN: With that wind off the water? I'm freezing.

TONY: I'm not. The mist almost looks like steam. Makes me feel warm.

EVAN *sits.*

EVAN: Ha! Warm? One dip in that water you'd change your mind. It'd freeze the balls right off ya!

TONY: I think my balls are safe.

EVAN: Mine aren't. Sometimes a man needs a little help to keep 'em warm.

He takes out a flask, nudges TONY *proudly, and takes a swig.*

EVAN: Aaaah! There's that warm glow. Here! Have a swig!

He nudges TONY *again with the flask, offering it.* TONY *shakes his head and moves away.*

TONY: No thanks.

EVAN: Suit yourself.

He takes another swig and looks around.

EVAN: Not very smart to be down here alone in the middle of the night.

TONY: I just came down here to sit for a while.

TONY *sits.*

EVAN: Alone? In the dark? Man, someone could just come by and...

He makes a knife gesture across his throat followed by a choking sound.

EVAN: Sure, I could be a murderer or something.

TONY: Are you?

EVAN: Now, if I was a murderer do you think I'd tell ya?

TONY: I dunno, I haven't met too many murderers.

EVAN: I'm just sayin', it's not the safest place.

TONY: I can take care of myself.

EVAN: Well, y'know, there's security around here. Better be careful or you could end up in the drunk tank. Unless of course you're lookin' for something.

TONY: Lookin' for something?

EVAN: Yeah...lookin' for something.

He makes a "hand-job" motion.

TONY: What? No!

EVAN: Don't act so shocked. It *is* the east end of Water Street in the middle of the night.

TONY: Is that what you're looking for?

EVAN: Me? Nah. I was just walkin' by. Headed home where it's warm. Same place you should be going.

TONY: You can go. I'm gonna stay a bit longer.

EVAN: So you can go on lookin' at the water?

TONY: Yeah.

EVAN: Okay. Suit yourself. Go on lookin' at the water.

TONY: Thanks.

TONY *goes back to looking out at the water and then realizes* EVAN *isn't moving.*

TONY: Thanks.

EVAN: No problem.

TONY: So, I'm good.

EVAN *looks at the sky.*

EVAN: Me too!

TONY: If you wanna get out of the cold—

EVAN: Y'know, you're right. It is kinda nice down here.

TONY: When it's quiet.

EVAN: Fine with me.

EVAN *stays seated.*

TONY: I meant—

EVAN: Sssssh. I'm lookin' at the water.

TONY: You weren't even here to—

EVAN: Shhhh. You just look at your side. I'll look at mine.

EVAN *looks out at the water. He takes another swig from his flask.*

Pause.

TONY: I really came down here to be by myself.

EVAN: That's okay. You can pretend I'm not even here.

EVAN *takes a bigger swig.*

EVAN: ...ahhh!

TONY *looks, then goes back to looking at the water.*
EVAN *takes another swig that goes down the wrong way.*
He coughs and shakes his head.

EVAN: Man, that gotta kick! Wow!

TONY: I don't believe this.

EVAN: Oh, sorry. You wanna swig now?

TONY: No.

EVAN: C'mon, it'll warm you up!

TONY: I'm not cold.

EVAN: Then why are your teeth chattering? C'mon!

EVAN *holds out flask.*

EVAN: This is what ya call a gin skin. Trust me, you'll like
gin.

TONY: I've had gin before. Many times.

EVAN: *(mocking)* Yeah, sure you have..."many times."
You sound like a sixteen-year-old with a fake ID.

TONY: I have. My partner, it was...her favourite drink.
Had it all the time.

EVAN: Well...she has good taste. But I bet you've never had
a gin skin before. Here...it's warm.

EVAN *offers the flask again and* TONY *takes it.*

EVAN: Go ahead.

TONY *takes a small sip.*

EVAN: Aw, take a bigger swig than that.

TONY *takes a bigger swig.*

EVAN: There ya go!

TONY: Tastes sweet.

EVAN: That's the honey.

TONY: It really does warm you up, hey?

EVAN: Just a nice, warm, gentle glow.

EVAN *takes the flask back, toasts* TONY.

EVAN: I'm Evan by the way.

Pause.

TONY: Tony.

Pause.

EVAN: So Tony, what do you do? I mean, besides hang out on the waterfront waitin' to get mugged?

TONY: You mean, like, for a living?

EVAN: Yeah.

TONY: I'm a writer.

EVAN: Oh yeah? Like a reporter?

TONY: No, more like—

EVAN: Like poetry and shit?

TONY: Yeah, something like that.

EVAN *nods. Awkward pause.*

EVAN: I'm in construction. In case you were wondering.

TONY: Like building houses and that type of "shit"?

EVAN: Yeah. Well, more like telling other people how to build the houses rather than swinging a hammer myself.

TONY *nods. Awkward pause.*

EVAN: Can I ask, what happened to your partner?

TONY: What makes you think anything happened?

EVAN: You said gin "used" to be her favourite drink.

TONY: Yeah.

EVAN: She quit drinking?

TONY: No.

EVAN: Ah! You broke up?

TONY: No.

Pause. EVAN *takes another swig from his flask. Silence.*

EVAN: Y'know, I saw you earlier.

TONY: Where?

EVAN: At the bar.

TONY: What bar?

EVAN: (*teasing*) Y'know...the "bar."

TONY: I was at a lot of bars tonight.

EVAN: I was only at the one. I like my routine. The back table with the lava lamp, that's my spot. You can see the whole bar from there. You looked like you were having an okay time.

TONY: You were watching me?

EVAN: Couldn't help it. You're a bit hard to miss.

TONY *looks down at his legs.*

TONY: Yeah, I guess I am.

EVAN: I wasn't talkin' about your crutches. I meant, you're a pretty good-lookin' guy.

TONY: Oh. Thanks.

EVAN: I saw you come in. I was gonna come over. But someone beat me to it.

TONY: You saw that?

EVAN: Yeah. He looked pretty cute.

TONY: So you're—

EVAN: I got a three-dollar bill in my back pocket.

TONY: Huh.

EVAN: What's the huh?

TONY: Nothing. I just didn't think you were...I mean you didn't strike me as a guy who's—

EVAN: What? Gay?

TONY: Yeah.

EVAN: Why not?

TONY: I dunno.

EVAN: Tell me.

TONY: Just...you look more like you came from a week in the woods than from a gay bar.

EVAN: (*amused*) Always with the butch thing. I don't wear a sequined spandex shirt downtown so I'm butch. No one even appreciates my soft hands.

TONY: I shouldn't have said anything.

EVAN: Aw, c'mon. You started this.

TONY: I just didn't think you were...I mean, you're a guy... appearing out of the dark on Water Street...looking a bit—

EVAN: Rough?

TONY: Yeah. I thought maybe you were—

EVAN: What? Here to swipe your wallet? Maybe a straight thug here to rough up a "fag"? I'm not. But it happens down here. Trust me. I know. Why I don't hang out here by myself.

Pause.

TONY: He. My partner. He. Not she. I wasn't sure—

EVAN: How I'd react? I get the caution. Especially down here. Why don't we get out of here? Grab a cab?

TONY: I don't think I'm in the mood for that anymore. But thanks.

EVAN: No man, I'm not trying to pick you up. Just trying to get you out of the cold.

TONY: Oh...yeah...stupid me.

EVAN: So, c'mon...c'mon—

TONY: What do you really want? 'Cause if it's money, I don't have any.

EVAN: I don't want your fucking money. Is it so hard to believe I could just be a nice guy wanting to help?

TONY: Who said I needed help?

EVAN: I just saw you sitting here and—

TONY: And assumed you had to stop and help the poor guy on crutches. Do your good deed?

EVAN: I stopped to help a GUY out from freezing his ass off. From being mugged. I stopped to be a friend.

TONY: I'm not looking for a "friend."

Pause.

EVAN: Okay...okay...

EVAN *goes to leave. He's almost gone when* TONY's *voice stops him.*

TONY: People are assholes!

EVAN: You meet an asshole tonight?

TONY: Yeah. It's like they seek me out.

EVAN *comes back.*

EVAN: Nah. They're everywhere.

TONY: I'm an easy target.

EVAN: I wouldn't take it too personally. To be fair, most assholes don't even know they're assholes. It's part of the whole..."assholishness."

Silence from TONY.

EVAN: It's true. Growing up, my friends always thought they were "great buddies." They weren't. They threw around insults every day like..."you fag," "that's so gay," "take it up the ass." I couldn't say anything, of course. I would just laugh. They didn't know they were being assholes. They were. But they didn't know it.

And then the questions. "Evan, why don't you have a girlfriend? Are you seeing anyone? When you gonna settle down, Evan?" I couldn't answer. "Gay" was a dirty word in my house, and any day I was sure I would be found out. I always felt like I was suffocating till I moved out.

TONY: Shale Harbour was pretty suffocating too. But I had the perfect cover.

TONY *shows his crutches.*

TONY: A guy on crutches? A sex life isn't exactly the first thing that comes to people's minds.

EVAN: Yup! More assholes! When did you get out?

TONY: I moved to town for university when I was like twenty.

EVAN: Ticket to freedom!

TONY *shakes his head.*

TONY: I was pretty green. I didn't even know gay bars existed till I moved out here. Social life in Shale Harbour? You bum smokes outside O'Brien's store, bingo at the parish hall, or beer and darts in Lahey's shed.

EVAN: When I moved out, I used to go to the bar all the time. It hasn't changed.

TONY: Drama...attitudes...eyes looking you up and down.

EVAN: But still the cheapest drinks in town. Plus, I have discovered the right approach to life to avoid that other crap. Fuck it. And fuck anyone who thinks I need their approval.

TONY: (*amused*) You sound like Jonathan.

EVAN: That your partner?

TONY: Yeah. That was his way of dealing with things. I'd always be the one worried what people thought. But Jonathan, he'd just say—

EVAN & TONY: Fuck it.

EVAN: Jonathan sounds like my kind of guy.

TONY *stays silent and observes* EVAN.

TONY: He died. A little over three years ago.

EVAN: I'm sorry.

TONY: (*formally*) Thank you.

Pause.

EVAN: Were you guys together long?

TONY: Nine years.

EVAN: Wow. A long time. Was he from town?

TONY: Oh yeah. He's what you would call a true townie.

EVAN: World stops beyond the overpass, hey?

TONY: Yeah. He used to ask me if we even had plumbing in Shale Harbour. He'd drive me crazy with that stuff all the time. On purpose.

EVAN: A good sense of humour, huh?

TONY: He was funny. Not like in-your-face funny, more—

EVAN: Subtle?

TONY: Yeah.

EVAN: How'd you meet?

TONY: At first we always used to see each other at "the bar."

EVAN: Nothing more romantic than locking eyes through the blow-up dildos and drag queens.

TONY: Something like that.

EVAN: Nine years. Must've been hard to lose him.

TONY: It was.

EVAN: Was it sudden?

TONY: Yes.

EVAN: Can I ask what—

TONY: (*firmly*) I don't really wanna talk about Jonathan anymore.

EVAN: Oh hey, that's fair.

Both men sit and look at the water in awkward silence. EVAN *breaks the silence.*

EVAN: You didn't have a good time at the bar tonight?

TONY: I dunno why I even went. I hadn't been there in about fifteen years. But, I figured, I'm single again. I'm gay. So that's what you do, right? You go to "the gay bar." The ONLY gay bar.

EVAN: From where I was sitting it looked like you were havin' an okay time.

TONY: You're not a very good observer, are ya?

EVAN: You were smiling for a bit. Out among people. Something you don't seem to do anymore.

TONY: How do you know what I do or don't do?

Pause.

EVAN: I've seen you around before. Some friends of some friends know you.

TONY: So, you know me?

EVAN: I know OF you.

TONY: St. John's...

EVAN: No matter how big it gets, everybody still knows your business like it was a town of twenty. Someone is always someone's cousin's father once removed who knew your mother. I've freaked you out, haven't I?

TONY: No, I love being stalked.

EVAN: Can I be honest with you?

TONY: You haven't been?

EVAN: I didn't just wander by on my way home. I followed you.

TONY: You what?

EVAN: But I swear I'm not some psycho or freak or anything.

TONY: No? Then why don't you just get out of here?

EVAN: Look, I'm not here to hurt you.

He approaches. TONY *raises a crutch.*

TONY: Just back off!

EVAN *steps back.*

EVAN: OKAY! I just saw you at the bar having an okay time, then next thing I know you're beatin' it out of there, upset. I grabbed my jacket to go ask you if you were okay but, despite those crutches, I couldn't keep up with ya. There you were, trudging through the snow down Water Street, not paying attention to cars or walk signals. You know you almost got knocked down twice?

TONY: As you can see, I'm fine.

EVAN: What got you so upset back there?

TONY: It doesn't matter.

EVAN: Why don't...why don't I get you a cab and you can go home?

TONY: 'Cause I don't wanna go home.

EVAN: You'd rather just hang out down here in the freezing cold all night?

TONY: Yes.

EVAN: Troubles at home?

TONY: No.

EVAN: Don't want to go back to an empty house?

TONY: Who says my house is empty? Or have you already staked that out too?

EVAN: Look, you don't need to tell me anything. But I'm not leaving you here alone.

TONY: Why? What difference does it make to you what I do or don't do?

EVAN: I'm just not leaving you here.

TONY: This is stupid. I don't even know you.

EVAN: I can still help.

TONY: God! Why does everyone assume I need help. I'm fine. I just came down here to sit down and look at the water.

Pause.

EVAN: I bet it was hard going to the bar tonight without Jonathan.

TONY: Who are you? Barbara Walters? This is none of your business. You don't know me and you wouldn't understand.

Pause.

EVAN: No. I can't imagine what that must be like, losing your partner. The closest I've ever come is losing my mom. That was hell. I can't imagine what you went through. What you're probably still going through.

TONY: I'm sorry. I'm sorry about your mom.

EVAN *steps to edge of dock, looks up at sky.* TONY *steps next to* EVAN *and also looks up.*

EVAN: It always amazes me. We all look at the same sky. We could be only ten feet away from each other and someone could be having the time of their life while someone else's life is falling apart and you'd never know it.

TONY: People enjoying themselves, used to make me so mad.

EVAN: Doesn't matter where you are, always feels like someone is missing. That you're all alone. Even in a room full of people.

TONY: Like a crowded bar.

EVAN: It's not true what they say, is it? Time heals? I thought I'd feel different by now, I wouldn't still feel so—

TONY: Empty.

EVAN: Empty. I think the worst time was the first Christmas without my Mom. Everyone decking the halls... partying...happy. I just wanted to go to bed and wait for it all to be over.

TONY: I hate Christmas. I remember early on, after Jonathan died, I had to go to a work Christmas party. I did *not* want to go. But everyone said it would be "good for me." You wanna know what the most upsetting thing of the night was? The buffet table.

EVAN: No meatballs?

TONY: At these things, Jonathan always used to walk in front of me holding both our plates, and I would load them up. I couldn't carry them but I could definitely make sure we had enough food. We loved to eat. This time, I went up to the buffet table, picked up one plate and just stood there. Alone. What do I do now? Everyone else was a couple. With someone. I ended up trailing at the end of the line by myself struggling to balance my plate. The walk back to the table was pretty long.

EVAN: I always feel awkward at those things. It's kinda why I keep a flask of gin close to my chest. A little bit of liquid courage. Maybe that's what you needed tonight?

TONY: I don't think it would've made a difference. Tonight was a mistake. I knew it as soon as I walked in. Hearing that booming music. All those guys staring, looking me up and down. I wanted to run. But I took a deep breath and kept walking.

Lights change to strobe dance floor lights. Sound: dance music. EVAN *watches the scene.*

EVAN: You did look a little nervous.

TONY: I didn't recognize any faces. It was pretty crowded. I tried to navigate to the bar. People looked and quickly made a path when they saw me. It was like the parting of the Red Sea. I grabbed a beer and went and found a space by the wall to lean and just...people-watch.

EVAN: *(laughing)* "People-watch." HA! You were cruising.

TONY: I was people-watching.

EVAN: You were "looking." Nothing wrong with that. That's when I was going to come over. But I missed my chance.

CARL *enters. He's attractive in a sweater and jeans. A "boy next door" type.*

CARL: Hey. 'Sup?

TONY: Hi.

CARL: 'Sup?

EVAN: Not much of a conversationalist, is he?

TONY: *(to* CARL*)* Just havin' a drink—enjoying the music.

CARL: Haven't seen ya here before.

TONY: No, I haven't been here in years.

CARL: Well, welcome back.

He raises his beer bottle to TONY.

TONY: Thanks.

CARL: What's your name?

TONY: Tony.

CARL: Carl. Nice to meet ya, Tony.

TONY: You too.

CARL: So, I had to come over and just tell ya how touched I am to see you down here, bud.

TONY: What do you mean?

CARL: I just want you to know I realize it takes a lot of effort for you to get down here. It's cool to see you here with everyone else. Good on ya, buddy!

He raises his beer to TONY.

TONY: Um...thanks.

CARL: No problem, bud! Like I said, it's good to see you down here. I'm impressed. Just one word of advice, hey? Most guys here are just looking for one thing, so be careful.

TONY: One thing?

CARL: Yeah, y'know, a one-night stand. A hookup. Just be careful.

TONY: Maybe that's what I'm looking for.

CARL: *(laughing)* That's funny. You're funny too. You seem like a good guy, buddy. I'd like to hang out with you sometime. And don't worry, this doesn't bother me.

The crutches and that, I've seen a lot worse. I'm studying to be a nurse so I've seen pretty much everything. I don't judge. What happened to you anyways?

TONY: Nothing. I was born like this.

CARL: Oh...really? Wow.

TONY: I think I'm gonna go.

CARL: What? Why? C'mon bud, let's go sit down!

TONY: I'm...I'm gonna go.

CARL: Are you serious? You're kidding me, right?

He calls out to TONY *as he's leaving.*

CARL: Y'know, you should be grateful!

CARL *throws up his arms and walks away.*

Lights switch back to waterfront.

EVAN: Some guy was an asshole. So what?

TONY: The minute he said he was impressed I could make it into a bar he reminded me when people see me for the first time, they see a guy on crutches. Not just a guy. A guy on crutches.

EVAN: You are a guy on crutches.

TONY: His comment about being "impressed" I was at the bar, that's not something to be impressed about. It's not a compliment.

EVAN: I think you are putting too much stock in what he—

TONY: And then, then he just assumes there is no possible way I could be looking to hook up. No possibility I just might have a raging hard-on in my pants. 'Cause y'know what? Guys on crutches don't have dicks.

EVAN: I don't think everyone—

TONY: He could've been a jerk about anything, but he went right for the disability. Hell, I would've been happier if he told me my shirt was ugly.

EVAN *tugs on* TONY's *shirt, laughing.*

EVAN: Your shirt is ugly.

TONY: Yeah, go ahead and laugh. You don't have to live it.

EVAN: You gotta laugh, Tony.

TONY: It's not funny!

EVAN: So, you're down here on the dock by yourself because some guy, who you don't even know, was a prick? That's pretty sad.

TONY: Thanks for your sympathy.

EVAN: I give sympathy when it's deserved, not when someone is having a pity party.

TONY: Typical. It's my fault, right? I should keep a stiff upper lip? Triumph over the barriers? Anything less and I'm not the inspirational story everyone expects, right? I'm just pitying myself.

EVAN: You're overreacting to a stupid incident with just one guy.

TONY: He just said what everyone else was thinking.

EVAN: Oh, so now y'know what everyone is thinking, hey? You're giving humanity a bad rap based on one guy. Everyone does not see you as just "a guy on crutches."

TONY: You ran after me 'cause you were worried about "the guy on crutches" beatin' it down the street.

EVAN: I would've run after you crutches or not.

TONY: Really? So, if a guy, not on crutches, just left a bar suddenly you would run after him?

EVAN: If he was hot, sure.

TONY: All a big joke isn't it?

EVAN: I ran after you. Excuse me for caring.

TONY: The fact is, you saw me as someone different. Someone you assumed needed help.

EVAN: Don't tell me how I see you. Yeah, I don't see you like other people. Why do you assume that's a bad thing? And what about Jonathan?

Pause.

TONY: What about Jonathan?

EVAN: You guys were together for—

TONY: Nine years.

EVAN: Nine years. That's a pretty long time to just be "helping" someone.

TONY: Jonathan was different.

EVAN: I'm sure he was.

TONY: Anyone around us who would say "help him!", he would just say: "Why? He can do it." He was blind to it.

EVAN: You must miss that.

TONY: When that guy couldn't imagine me in any kind of sexual way—he actually laughed at the idea I might be looking to hook up...I just felt so—

EVAN: Do you know, one time some guy came up to me and said I'd be really hot if it wasn't for the bags underneath my eyes. See?

EVAN *points under his eyes.* TONY *looks.*

TONY: They're not bad.

EVAN: Please, they're overweight luggage.

TONY *chuckles.*

EVAN: And for the record, you are cute!

TONY: Thanks. I miss having someone telling me I'm "cute."

EVAN: Nothing better for the ego.

TONY: I can think of one thing better for the ego.

EVAN: Oooooh really? So what exactly *were* you looking for tonight?

TONY: I guess a...just a...y'know.

EVAN: You can say it. A "hookup." You were looking for a hookup. Nothing wrong with getting back in the game with a hookup. First night out, a romantic thing like you had with Jonathan isn't gonna just fall in your lap.

TONY: Um...well...I dunno if you would call our first encounter particularly romantic.

Light shifts. TONY *starts air-typing. Sound of keys clicking.* EVAN *gets up and looks over* TONY's *shoulder. Sound: the beeps of incoming messages.*

TONY: He said "hey" to me...mmm....

TONY *types.*

TONY: Hi!

EVAN: His name is Sedarisguy?

TONY: Yeah, Jonathan was a big reader.

EVAN: A man with intelligence. I like it.

Messenger beep.

TONY: *(reading)* How's it going?

TONY *types.*

TONY: Good. Thanks. You?

TONY *clicks to send. Pause. Messenger beep.*

TONY: *(reading)* Good. A bit horny.

EVAN: Nothing like getting to the point.

TONY *types.*

TONY: Me too...LOL.

TONY *clicks to send. Pause. Messenger beep.*

TONY: *(reading)* I like your profile. You are pretty hot.

TONY *types.*

TONY: Thanks! You are too!

TONY *clicks to send. Pause. Messenger beep.*

TONY: *(reading)* I've seen you around town before. Oh great...what does he mean by that?

TONY *types.*

TONY: Um...you have?

TONY *clicks to send. Pause. Messenger beep.*

TONY: *(reading)* Yeah, at the bar mostly. You are one sexy man.

EVAN: He's got it bad.

TONY *types.*

TONY: Thanks. I think I've seen you there too. You usually come in with a group and sit in the back, right?

TONY *clicks to send. Pause. Messenger beep.*

TONY: *(reading)* Yeah that's me.

What does the smiley winky face mean?

TONY *types.*

TONY: So...hmm...hmm...so you know about my... "situation"? No. *(he deletes)* My..."physique"? No, that's stupid. *(he deletes)* My "crutches"? Oh yeah that sounds sexy. *(he deletes)* My...my..."physicality"?

TONY *clicks to send. Pause. Messenger beep.*

TONY: *(reading)* Yeah, you are hot!

TONY *types.*

TONY: You are hotter!

Clicks. Pause. Messenger beep.

TONY: *(reading)* Can you travel?

TONY *types.*

TONY: Yup!

Clicks. Messenger beep.

TONY: What are you doing tonight?

TONY *types.*

TONY: Seeing you.

Clicks. Beep.

TONY: *(reading)* Come over.

TONY *types.*

TONY: On my way!

Clicks.

Light shifts.

EVAN: Wow! That was fucking poetry!

TONY: It was the first time I was with someone who didn't ask any questions. Didn't wonder if I could...

EVAN: If you could what?

TONY: If I could...

EVAN: What?

TONY: Perform.

EVAN: That's what we're calling it? (*mocking*) "Perform." Perform what? A hand-job? Sucking dick? Flying on a trapeze? What?

TONY: You know what I mean. All of my life I've been told it's what's inside that counts. But sometimes...sometimes you need to know that you're wanted. Jonathan was the first guy who ever did that for me. I mean, TOTALLY did that for me.

EVAN: Gay courtship straight-up. Sex before the relationship. Any gay guy tells you he has never, in his life, hooked up like that before...he's lying.

TONY: I thought the shallowness of it was great. I know it makes me sound kinda superficial.

EVAN: You sound human.

Pause.

TONY *looks over to* EVAN.

TONY: I'm Paul.

EVAN: Excuse me?

PAUL: My name. It's Paul, not Tony. I dunno why I lied.

EVAN: Probably 'cause you were approached by a shady stranger down on the waterfront.

PAUL: I don't think you're shady anymore.

EVAN: Well, good. Now, give me your money!

PAUL: What?

EVAN: Hey, just kidding...Paul.

They both smile. Pause.

EVAN: Those must've been some pretty hot hookups if you're still talkin' about 'em.

PAUL: He was just so handsome, y'know? He had these deep brown eyes. This crooked little smile when he was up to something. A sexy hairy chest and...well...his...

EVAN: His what?

PAUL: He was just...he was...well-proportioned.

EVAN: You mean he had a big...?

EVAN *lifts up his hands to approximate a measurement.* PAUL *reaches over and widens them.*

EVAN: You're exaggerating.

PAUL: Nope!

EVAN: Well, I'm sure Jonathan appreciates the admiration. So you guys had great sex, huh?

PAUL: I can't believe I'm talking about this. Yeah. After a while, things started running a bit deeper.

EVAN: Even I can't imagine casual sex for nine years. Nobody is that good. *(boasting)* Well, almost nobody. What happened to make you guys take the leap from casual fuck buddies?

PAUL: Shakespeare.

EVAN: To fuck or not to fuck? Was that the question?

PAUL: We'd probably known each other for six months and Jonathan finally asked me if I would like to go grab a coffee sometime. I dunno if he expected me to say yes, but I did. And we actually made plans. He wanted to get coffee on Sunday and I told him I had to spend the day trying to memorize a whole Shakespearean sonnet. I was doing this playwriting course at the time.

EVAN: You write plays?

PAUL: I try. Anyways, for our final assignment we had to memorize and perform a classic scene and then write and perform an original scene. I'm okay with speaking in class, but when it comes to memorization I suck, big time. And Jonathan offered to help me.

It was May, so we made plans to go to the park with some coffees and a blanket and memorize my Shakespeare piece. I thought he was going to think I was an idiot. Shakespeare...it's so hard. But he just sat with me, for eight hours.

Pause.

PAUL: There was this one line I just could never get, no matter how many times Jonathan went over it with me, but he was so patient.

EVAN: What was the line you had so much trouble with?

PAUL: Oh god. It was so long ago. Something about "thou perceives love more strong"—

EVAN: "This thou perceivest, which makes thy love more strong, To love that well which thou must leave ere long."

PAUL: That's it! How do you know that?

EVAN: *(impressed with himself)* Y'know what? I'm not quite sure. Sonnet 73. I guess some things just stick with you.

PAUL: You don't strike me—

EVAN: As a guy who knows Shakespeare? Still judging me, hey? Can you say the line?

Slowly, over the following, lights change to a warm sunny glow. Sounds of birds chirping, children laughing.

PAUL: Oh God...no...I can't remember that.

EVAN: C'mon. *(coaching)* "This thou perceivest..."

PAUL: *(remembering)* "This thou perceivest..."

EVAN: "...which makes thy love more strong."

PAUL: "...which makes thy love more strong."

EVAN: "To love that well which..."

PAUL: "To love that well which..."

EVAN: "...thou must leave ere long."

PAUL: "...thou must leave ere long."

EVAN: "Good! Now, let's hear it all together!"

PAUL *pauses. Takes a deep breath. Clears his throat.*

PAUL: "Perceive this—"

EVAN: "This thou..."

PAUL: "This thou perceivest..."

EVAN *coaxes, drawing the words out of* PAUL's *mouth.*

EVAN: "Which makes..."

PAUL: "Which makes thy...thy..."

EVAN *crosses hands across chest.*

PAUL: Love! "Which makes thy love more..."

EVAN *raises arms up in a strong man pose.*

PAUL: Strong! "Which makes thy love more strong!"...um...

EVAN *holds up two fingers and then does the love crossing hands over his chest again.*

PAUL: Peace? Love?

EVAN *repeats the action more sternly.*

PAUL: Two! To love! "To love that well which thou must..."

EVAN *acts as if he's leaving.*

PAUL: You're running...you're running away...you're leaving! "To love that well which though must leave ere... ere..."

EVAN *pretends he's measuring a short stick and then a long stick between his arms. The gestures are similar to those used earlier when describing Jonathan.*

PAUL: Penis?

EVAN *puts his hands down in frustration. He then puts them up again, showing his hands going from short to long.*

PAUL: Short...long...long! "To love that well which thou must leave ere LONG!"

EVAN *applauds Paul.*

EVAN: You still got it in there.

Lights switch back to waterfront.

PAUL *walks away from* EVAN.

PAUL: *(laughing)* That was a good day.

EVAN: There'll be other good days.

Silent pause from PAUL.

EVAN: Tonight...tonight was just one night. I bet most people are very accepting. Fuck that guy Carl.

PAUL: I hate that word.

EVAN: What? Fuck?

PAUL: "Accepting." From the day I was born I was always someone who had to be accepted. Back in Shale Harbour, I wasn't just a little boy. I was the crippled little boy.

I remember being like four years old and people would describe me as crippled. I didn't even know what that meant. I looked it up in the dictionary once: "To become unable to move or walk properly. Something flawed or imperfect." I got it. I wasn't like everyone else. After that, I always felt like everyone was "accepting" me.

EVAN: We're all flawed. Hell, if I made a list for myself we'd be here all night. Who cares what people thought when you were a kid? You said you went to university. You're supporting yourself. You're not homeless. You sound intelligent enough.

PAUL: When I walk down the street, meet new people, get approached by a guy in a bar, everyone still sees "the cripple." I never should've left Shale Harbour.

EVAN: You don't mean that.

PAUL: I wouldn't have to keep proving myself. It would've been safe.

EVAN: A little town where everyone called you crippled doesn't sound safe to me.

PAUL: Everyone knew me. I was "little Paul," the crippled boy who lives up the road. No explanations needed. No awkward questions. No stares from strangers. Every day I'd know what to expect. My parents being overprotective. Neighbours yelling, "Wait for little Paul!" as the other kids ran down to the beach. Everyone patting my head as they said, "God love 'im!" Always getting five dollars.

EVAN: Five dollars? What were you, a stripper?

PAUL: No. I was "special." I used to get handed money. Walking through a store, down the street, adults would just stop and give me five dollars. I thought it was great. Hey, it's five dollars. That's a lot of money to a kid. My mom didn't like it. She kept telling me I shouldn't take it. "Don't take it!" I didn't understand why. Why would I turn down free money?

It wasn't until years later I understood. Why I shouldn't take it. She was teaching me self-respect. That money was being given out of pity. "Oh, that's a sin, I'll give him money." It's like being congratulated by someone 'cause you made it into a bar by yourself.

Pause.

EVAN: After my mom died, my Dad had a hard time dealing with us kids. We got shipped off to uncles and aunts like a travelling orphan roadshow. And relatives, teachers, neighbours, they all had that same look, "those poor children." I think that's where I got my "fuck you" attitude. Even after we moved back home with my Dad, we were still the sad story of the neighbourhood. Pitied.

What? Why are you looking at me like that?

PAUL: Nothing. It just sounds like—

EVAN: Sounds like what?

Pause.

PAUL: *(changing the subject)* I bet you don't like to talk about it very much either.

EVAN: It's not exactly fuzzy warm childhood memories. Everyone wanting to "save us." I hated their sanctimonious charitable bullshit. Judging me. Assuming I needed to be saved.

PAUL: Or not saved. I was born premature. They didn't even know if I was gonna make it. A nun told my mom she should pray I died 'cause I'd be better off in God's arms. I'd be better off dead rather than face a life the way I was.

EVAN: How do you know that?

PAUL: I was back home visiting a couple of weeks ago.

Mom was playing cards with Mrs. O'Brien and Aunt Vicky. They were talking about kids and grandkids. I was in the TV room off the kitchen. I heard the whole thing.

You hear someone is having a baby and it's all cute and celebrating. Everybody hopes for a healthy baby. And everybody celebrates when the baby is healthy. I can't help think, when I was born, did people celebrate?

EVAN: Who cares what that nun said. You amounted to something. I'm sure it wasn't easy, but whose life is? You gotta just...you gotta just keep proving assholes wrong. Keep fighting.

PAUL: I thought I was done fighting.

Pause.

When it looked like me and Jonathan weren't just dating, that we were together, partners, I didn't feel like I had to fight anymore. I could breathe. I found that sense of belonging I'd searched my whole life for. Complete unconditional love for who I was and how I looked. And now...now I'm back to where I was. Alone. Except, I don't have that same fight in me. I'm tired. I'm just...tired.... I'm done.

EVAN: We don't get to choose when we're done. What're you gonna do about it, hey?

PAUL *remains silent.*

EVAN: I asked you a question. What are you going to do about it?

PAUL: I dunno.

EVAN: I saw you. Earlier. I saw you. Standing on the edge here—

PAUL: I dunno what you're talkin' about.

EVAN: Didn't think you were a coward.

PAUL: I'm not a coward.

EVAN: Really? But you don't know what I'm talkin' about? If you're gonna sit here and say "fuck you" to anyone and everyone who cares about you, at least have the guts to admit what you're doin' down here.

PAUL: It's none of your business what I'm doing.

EVAN: I'm making it my business.

PAUL: What? You think 'cause you've been talking to me for a half hour you have some right to tell me how to live my life?

EVAN: That's your problem. You're not living it. You don't want to live it. Do you?

PAUL: Stop it!

EVAN: Paul, I know what it feels like when things are a bit rough—

PAUL: A bit rough?

EVAN: I didn't mean it like that.

PAUL: You don't have a clue what you're talkin' about. You leave here and you get to walk up the street, no help needed. You can even go back to the bar. Bound up over those stairs. Glide in unnoticed. Stare eye to eye with people you talk to instead of up at them. Or them down at you.

EVAN: I know I don't totally know what it's like to—

PAUL: Easy isn't it? Doling out advice?

EVAN: I can help you.

PAUL: I don't want your help! Do me a favour? Take your Good Samaritan act to someone else. Go be a hero to some other guy.

Pause.

EVAN: So you're just gonna fall into the ocean, hey? Just gently float away from it all? Into that misty water you said looks so warm. Looks so inviting, doesn't it?

PAUL *is silent. He avoids eye contact.*

EVAN: That's not what it's gonna be like. You're gonna hit that fucking freezing water and your body's gonna go into shock. Your heart is gonna slow. You'll be numb, unable to move. And then you'll sink. And just when you think it can't get any worse—you're out of air. You can't hold your breath anymore, so you start breathing. Breathing in water. Filling your lungs so they feel like they're going to explode. There's no gentle, warm floating away, Paul. You just become a bloated, blue, frozen, half-eaten corpse that has to be dragged out of the water. So inviting.

PAUL *is silent.*

EVAN: Go ahead then—jump! What are you waitin' for? You mulling it over? You better be pretty sure what you really want. When you're dead, you're dead. No going back. I'll ask you again. Do you want to die? Answer me! You wanna die?

PAUL: It doesn't matter what I want. We don't get what we want. I didn't want him to die but he did. He died. He died and left me behind. And I'm so—

EVAN: Angry?

PAUL: Yes. ANGRY.

EVAN: At what?

PAUL: Everything.

EVAN: AT WHAT?

PAUL: AT HIM! For making me think the crutches, the deformed legs, the leg braces, the ugly scars from surgeries, that none of it mattered. He made me believe it didn't matter. And then he left. He left me, alone. And without being seen through his eyes, it all still matters. It matters every time I walk into a room full of strangers. It matters when someone looks at me. I mean, really looks at me. It matters when guys like Carl can make me feel like a fucking deformed outcast. I don't want this life anymore.

I wanna life where I know what it's like to run. To just jump out of bed in the morning without having to strap on hard metal splints that dig into my skin all day. A life where I'm just a guy. Like any other guy. Nothing to look at. Nothing to point at. No doors needing to be held open. No whispering. Just...normal.

Pause.

EVAN: Always about the disability with you, isn't it? The root of all your problems? The reason why you are alone down here wanting to check out?

He points to PAUL's *crutches.*

EVAN: Without this...

He points to PAUL's *legs.*

EVAN: ...and this, life would be worth living?

PAUL: Yes.

EVAN: Even without Jonathan?

Pause.

EVAN: You got it all figured out, huh? The great solution! Get rid of the crutches...the braces...everything would be fine? Nothing to hold you back? That's the issue?

PAUL: Yes.

Pause.

EVAN: *(gently)* Show me.

PAUL: Show you what?

EVAN: What it would be like. Obviously you've been thinking about it for a long time. So, how would it be?

PAUL: I can't show you.

EVAN: C'mon, you said you were a writer, so write. Use your imagination. How would it be? You'd probably still be heading out tonight. A night on the town. You gotta get ready. Do something with the hair...and this shirt.

PAUL: I like this shirt. It's a perfect downtown shirt.

EVAN: If you have a shirt that's only appropriate to wear when drinking down on George Street, it's not a good shirt.

PAUL: What should I wear, a suit and tie?

EVAN: Sure, why not?

PAUL: I am not wearing a tie.

EVAN: Are you ready?

PAUL: (*confidently*) I'm ready.

PAUL *makes his way up onto a pillar of the dock. He and* EVAN *stand approximately the same height now.*

EVAN: Well, look at you! I guess you won't be needing these anymore.

EVAN *takes* PAUL*'s crutches and places them out of the way.*

PAUL: I feel so different. So…"normal."

EVAN: And it's your big night out on the town, right? Same bar?

Lights change to downtown bar lighting. Dance music in the background.

EVAN: Place doesn't change much, hey? No matter what life you are living.

PAUL: No, it's different.

EVAN: How?

PAUL: I'm wearing regular size jeans that actually make my legs look long. And see…

He points down.

PAUL: Cowboy boots! I always wanted to wear cowboy boots, but I never could. They don't fit over leg braces.

EVAN: Ride 'em cowboy!

PAUL: And I actually left you in the dust going up over those stairs. No pausing at the bottom getting ready to hoist and balance myself with crutches one step at a time. Hell, I even managed to take the stairs two by two. And when I walked in, I looked at everyone eye to eye. Do you know how cool that is? To meet someone eye to eye rather than having to look up at them? And guys are staring back. But this time it's because they like what they see. I can feel it. Usually I am ready to bolt out of places like this. But tonight...tonight I feel like staying.

EVAN: Well, hold on to your cowboy boots, 'cause Carl should be headed your way...right...about...now.

CARL *enters and walks directly past* PAUL. *He hangs out further away surveying the room.*

PAUL: What was that?

EVAN: What?

PAUL: He just walked right past me.

EVAN: You are just one of the guys now. Blending into the crowd. Make up your mind, Paul, on what you want.

PAUL: You're right. I'm just one of the guys.

EVAN: Besides, don't write him off just yet. Maybe Carl is just shy. Needs a little encouragement.

EVAN *nudges* PAUL. PAUL *looks over at* CARL.

PAUL: He's not interested. Why don't we just go?

EVAN: Wait...did you see that?

PAUL: What?

EVAN: He just took a looooong look at you.

PAUL: No he didn't. Maybe he was looking at you.

EVAN: Trust me, he was not looking at me. I bet if you just gave him a little wave he'd come over.

PAUL: I'm not giving him a "little wave."

EVAN: Sure you are.

EVAN *makes* PAUL *wave.*

PAUL: Stop that! This is my scene.

EVAN: Here he comes.

CARL *slowly approaches.*

CARL: Hey there.

EVAN *nudges* PAUL.

PAUL: Hi.

CARL: How's your night going?

PAUL: Good thanks. You?

CARL: Not bad. Same old, same old down here.

PAUL: Yeah, the place hasn't changed much.

CARL: Oh, you've been here before? I've never seen you and I'm sure I would have noticed!

PAUL: I haven't been here in years.

CARL: Oh, well, welcome back!

He raises his beer to PAUL *and takes a sip.*

CARL: Name is Carl.

PAUL: Tony.

EVAN *coughs.*

PAUL: Uh...Paul.

CARL: Okay Tony-Paul. Nice to meet you.

PAUL: Um...you too.

CARL: So what brings you downtown tonight?

PAUL: Nothing really. Well, nothing in particular. Just... just wanted to get out of the house.

CARL: Same with me. Though I have to admit I dunno why I came here. I'd rather be having a quiet chat than spending time on a dance floor.

PAUL: Me too.

CARL: Although one good thing makes me glad I came here tonight.

PAUL: What's that?

CARL: I got to meet a cute guy.

CARL *gives* PAUL *a touch on the shoulder.*

PAUL: Heh...thanks.

CARL: Did you wanna get out of here? Maybe grab a coffee?

PAUL: Oh, well 1 wasn't planning on making it a late night.

CARL: Me neither. I have to work in the morning, unfortunately. Just a coffee and chat where it's a bit quieter?

PAUL: Maybe some other time. I'm getting pretty tired.

CARL: Oh. Okay. If you're sure?

PAUL: I'm sure.

CARL: Well, what if I give you my number? Maybe we could go for a coffee or something some other time?

PAUL: Um...yeah.

CARL *takes a business card out of his pocket.*

CARL: Well, here's my card. You can use that number or email me. I'm pretty free this week.

PAUL *takes the card and looks at it.*

PAUL: Well, I'm pretty busy the next little while—

CARL: *(defeated)* Oh. Well...yeah...sure. I get it. It was really nice meeting you, Tony-Paul.

PAUL: You too.

CARL *exits.*

Lights shift.

EVAN *hands* PAUL *his crutches.* PAUL *dismounts from pillar.*

EVAN: Wow! You blew it.

PAUL: It doesn't matter. Don't forget he was a jerk.

EVAN: He seemed pretty nice.

PAUL: This was a dumb idea.

EVAN: I found it pretty interesting. No leg braces. No crutches. You still ran away.

PAUL: I didn't run.

EVAN: You may as well have.

PAUL: When he started chatting, talking about going out, my heart started pounding. I could hear it in my ears. My face was hot, my mouth was dry. And the more he kept talking, the more I knew I just had to get out of there.

EVAN: But this time it wasn't about the disability, right? I think he said all the right things.

PAUL: Yeah...but I still knew he was a jerk.

EVAN: Maybe. Or maybe you're hiding.

PAUL: I'm not hiding.

EVAN: Your disability. I think on some level you like it.

PAUL: Oh yeah, I love it.

EVAN: Keeps you pretty safe. Your own little fortress. Anybody who tries to get in, tries to get to know you, well, they're just some asshole. It's pretty easy to walk away from an asshole. Poor old Carl didn't stand a chance.

PAUL: I told you what Carl, the real Carl, said to me. He WAS an asshole.

EVAN: You get that reaction all the time, hey?

PAUL: Yes! God, have you been listening to me?

EVAN: I've been listening. But have you? You hear what you wanna hear. What keeps you safe. I saw you do it.

Light shift. CARL *enters and approaches* PAUL.

CARL: 'Sup?

PAUL *nods, doesn't answer.*

CARL: 'Sup? How are you doing tonight?

PAUL: Good, thanks.

CARL: I noticed you coming in and just thought I'd say hi.

PAUL: Hi.

CARL: So I have to admit, I'm a bit nervous.

PAUL: Why?

CARL: I've never really come up to a guy like this before, but I saw you. I guess you looked more approachable than the other guys here.

PAUL: Because of the disability?

CARL: I guess...a bit. But I was more impressed with you walking into a bar by yourself. Especially this one. Good on ya, bud!

PAUL: What?

CARL: Just, I know it can be intimidating to walk in here on your own. Thought I would come over and help you out. Have a chat. Do you wanna sit down?

PAUL: No, I can stand. I don't need any "help."

CARL: Oh, hey, no. I know. That wasn't about your disability. I'm not judging. I don't have a problem with it.

PAUL: You don't have a problem with it? Well, thanks, that's good to know.

CARL: Sorry. That came out wrong...I haven't seen you here before...Are you from out of town?

PAUL: No, I live in town. I just haven't been at this bar in years.

CARL: Well, welcome back.

He toasts PAUL *with his beer.*

CARL: I would warn ya though to be a bit careful here by yourself. Most guys here are only looking for one thing.

PAUL: One thing?

CARL: Yeah, y'know, a hookup.

PAUL: Maybe that's what I'm looking for.

CARL: (*smiling, chuckling*) Nah. I don't think you're that type of guy. I can tell these things. Do you mind me asking...what happened? You don't have to answer.

PAUL: I was born like it.

CARL: Oh wow, that must've been hard. I only asked 'cause I'm studying to be a nurse. I've seen a lot of people overcome different things. I really respect that.

PAUL: Yeah...I'm gonna go.

CARL: What? Hey, I didn't mean to offend. Why don't we just go and sit down and talk? How about a beer? My treat!

PAUL: No, I'm just gonna go.

PAUL *walks away.*

CARL: Geez man...

CARL *exits.*

EVAN: Carl just wanted to chat. Get to know you. And you just walk away. 'Cause he's just an asshole with a hang-up. Talk about judging and rejection. Ever think maybe his heart was racing? Maybe he had anxiety that was going through the roof? That he felt awkward? Just 'cause you can't see someone's problems doesn't mean they're not there.

PAUL: I didn't know he felt like that.

EVAN: Because you heard what you wanted to hear. If he's a jerk about your disability it makes it easy to walk away.

PAUL: That's not what happened.

EVAN: That's exactly what happened.

PAUL: No it's not! I just...I just wasn't in the mood...I wasn't—

EVAN: You weren't what?

Silence from PAUL.

EVAN: Y'know, you're right. You are crippled. But it has nothing to do with your legs.

PAUL: SHUT UP! You have no right to talk to me that way. None!

EVAN: And what about Jonathan?

PAUL: What about him?

EVAN: Do you think this is what he would want for you?

PAUL: You don't know anything about Jonathan.

EVAN: I know he wouldn't want you to throw yourself into the ocean. To do yourself in. What do you think he would say to you right now?

PAUL: Stop! You leave Jonathan out of—

EVAN: You know EXACTLY what he would say to you! He'd ask you what in God's name are you doing down here? Paul, what're you doin'—

PAUL: It doesn't matter, does it? 'Cause he's not here. Is he?

EVAN: You tell me.

Pause.

EVAN: Why did you name me Evan, Paul?

PAUL: Because that's who you are. You're Evan, a stranger I meet on the waterfront.

EVAN: A stranger? A stranger whose mom died when he was young? Who was shipped around with his other siblings? Who can recite a Shakespeare sonnet you had to study off by heart? A stranger who can tell you're upset, even when you say you're not. A stranger who loves you, unconditionally. Who thinks you're beautiful. Paul, you know me, I'm—

PAUL: Jonathan.

Pause.

PAUL: It wasn't supposed to be you this time.

JONATHAN: Why am I here?

PAUL: Because it always turns out to be you. Over and over, it's the same story. No matter where I go. What I do. What I write. It always leads back to you.

JONATHAN: You used to be able to write about anything. The sky was the limit.

PAUL: Now it's different.

JONATHAN: Why?

PAUL: Because you're not here.

JONATHAN: You were writing long before I came along. You didn't need me to be creative. What about that comedy? The one about the two college roommates in the sixties? Nothing to do with me. Or the one in the diner with that guy coming out of the closet? Getting it on with a studly baseball player? That was definitely not about me.

PAUL: Every time I try to move on, go forward, do something new, I can't. I just keep going back. It just feels so...unfinished.

JONATHAN: What does?

PAUL: The way it happened.

JONATHAN *looks at* PAUL *in silence.*

PAUL: Do you...do you know what happened?

JONATHAN *shakes his head.*

PAUL: It was September 24. It was still really warm. Like summer. The leaves hadn't started turning. I remember the trees still being all green and full of life. It was a beautiful day. We both had just gotten home from work. I drove up to the driveway and there you were. Getting the groceries out of your trunk. Along with this toy truck.

Lights shift to a sunny late September evening. JONATHAN *and* PAUL *are outside their house.*

JONATHAN: Hey, Boo!

PAUL: Hey! What's the truck for?

JONATHAN: It's for the conference tomorrow. We promised we'd donate a kid's prize for the Christmas drive. It's from one of our distributors.

PAUL: It's nice.

JONATHAN: *(teasing)* You can't have it. I did bring you something though.

PAUL: You did?

JONATHAN: Yup! Close your eyes.

PAUL *closes his eyes and puts his hand out and* JONATHAN *places a chocolate orange in his hand.*

PAUL: Mmm, dark chocolate orange. Awesome. Thank you. Although I think you're trying to sabotage our diet.

JONATHAN: You can save it for our cheat night.

PAUL: Every night is our cheat night. How was your day?

JONATHAN: It was so great. I just had a two-hour conversation with Julia.

PAUL: Who's Julia?

JONATHAN: You don't listen to me. Remember...? From our HR office in Halifax...? Paul, you met her at the Christmas party last year.

PAUL: Oh yeah, Julia!

JONATHAN: You don't remember Julia.

PAUL: I don't remember Julia.

JONATHAN: Well, anyways, she's coaching me on how to be a better manager. What my goals should be. What kind of manager I wanna be.

PAUL: What kind of manager do you wanna be?

JONATHAN: More...personal, I guess. We talked about how sometimes I have these walls that keep me from getting too close to people. And that sometimes makes me come across as cold or uncaring. So we talked about how I could break down some of those walls.

PAUL: Sounds like a pretty serious conversation.

JONATHAN: Yeah, but it was really good. I trust her. I think they're grooming me for something.

PAUL: Really?

JONATHAN: Yeah! How does Ontario sound to you?

PAUL: You're getting transferred to Ontario?

JONATHAN: I hear Kitchener is beautiful!

PAUL: Kitchener? What the heck is in Kitchener?

JONATHAN: *(playfully)* Lots of kitchens I hear! Y'know, if I got transferred you could leave that job you hate. Spend some time just writing for yourself. Write a new play or something.

PAUL: You know all the right things to say, don't you? But that could be cool.

JONATHAN: Well, nothing's set in stone yet. So don't get too excited.

PAUL: *(proudly)* No, I bet you'll get it.

JONATHAN: Y'know when I was talking to Julia about my walls and stuff, I also talked about you.

PAUL: How great I am?

JONATHAN *chuckles and then moves closer to* PAUL.

JONATHAN: How I never let anyone in. That I used to think I didn't need anyone. I told her you just kept chipping away at me. That you're one of the few people who ever broke through my wall. And I told her how happy I was you did.

PAUL: I didn't know you felt like that.

JONATHAN: So...you gonna make dinner?

PAUL: Is that what all this is about? Trying to get me to make dinner? Yes, I'll make dinner.

JONATHAN: Okay. I'm gonna go use the bathroom and then get packed for my trip.

PAUL: What time is your flight in the morning?

JONATHAN: Five thirty. We'll have to leave here like four.

PAUL: Ugh.

JONATHAN: Hey, I brought you chocolate!

PAUL: Thank you. I'll put the chicken in the oven.

JONATHAN: Wanna watch the next episode of *Dr. Who*?

PAUL: Yes! I'll set it up.

JONATHAN: I'll be quick.

JONATHAN *goes to exit. He stops and turns towards* PAUL *in silence.*

Pause. Light slowly shifts.

PAUL: I thought you were just being slow. The alarm went off on the stove. The chicken was ready. I still remember that sound. It was like one of those little dings. Loud enough to hear from outside. *(sound: ding)* But I didn't go to the stove first. I went to call out to you. But I didn't. I just started walking up the stairs. Sixteen steps, one by one. *(ding)* The oven alarm was still going off and I was getting ready to yell, "You better hurry or the chicken is going to burn!" But I didn't.

I just knocked on the washroom door. You didn't answer. I didn't knock again. I didn't call out. I just turned the lock on the handle with my fingernail. I opened the door. *(ding)*

You were on the floor. Just lying there. I couldn't tell if you had passed out or fainted or what happened. You were just lying there with your eyes half-open. I could see those beautiful dark brown eyes. I looked and yelled, "Jonathan!" I couldn't tell if you were looking at me or not.

(*sound: phone dialling and ringing*) I phoned 911. They could barely make out what I was saying. They told me to start doing chest compressions. That they would be there. And for me to stay on the line.

I put the 911 operator on speaker and she told me to find the middle of your chest, clasp one hand over the other, and start pumping. I didn't tell her I had crutches. I didn't tell her that because of the leg braces I couldn't kneel. I just started pressing on your chest, like a push-up. I told her they better hurry because I didn't know how long I could keep that up. And she told me I had to. Me doing compressions was going to keep you alive till the paramedics got there. I had to keep you alive.

After a while, I got so tired. My arms were failing underneath me. She was counting. I had done four hundred and forty-six push-ups. I couldn't keep going. I begged her to tell them to hurry because I was getting so tired. She told me we were going to count to eight hundred. Another eight hundred chest compressions and then they should be there.

I was so tired. Eventually all I could do was keep pressing with one of my forearms. I knew I wasn't doing it right anymore. I told her they had to hurry. I collapsed. (*sound: sirens*) And then I heard the sirens. I still had to get down to unlock the door, but I was so tired. But I crawled down the stairs and to the door. I managed to crawl. That's when they went up to help. I kept asking them if you were breathing and all they would say was they were working on you. They wouldn't say yes. They wouldn't say you were breathing. Just that they were working on you. I knew. I didn't want to know. But I knew.

I didn't keep up the chest compressions. When it came down to the most important action of my life, I couldn't do it. I couldn't do it! Because I'm crippled!

JONATHAN: An aortic dissection. A weakness in the wall of the valve that supplies blood to the heart. It can tear at any time. And when it does, blood can no longer get to your heart. A defect from birth. You weren't the only one with a disability.

PAUL: If I had only been able to do it right. I let you down.

JONATHAN: Is that what you think?

PAUL: It's what I fear.

JONATHAN: You need to make peace with that. You need to move on.

PAUL: I've tried.

JONATHAN: Have you? Then why is this about me?

PAUL: It wasn't supposed to be. But no matter where I turn, you're there. I came across one of your shirts I kept. It was hanging in my closet. And I swear I could hear you down the hall ironing your pants and yelling, "Boo, I'll be ready in five minutes." Or I'm at the gym and I look over and for a split second I think I see you running on the treadmill. I find myself talking to you all the time like you're still here.

JONATHAN: But I'm not here.

House lights come up, as if the show has ended. PAUL *goes to centre stage and looks out to the audience and up to the tech booth.*

PAUL: Turn those lights back down...please? Turn those lights back down! It's not over!

JONATHAN: It's time, Paul.

PAUL: No. Let's keep it going just a little longer. I still have a scene.

PAUL *addresses the audience.*

PAUL: You'll all love it. Just give me five more minutes okay...please?

JONATHAN: Paul, it has to end.

PAUL: No! I have more. You...you come sit...come sit on the waterfront.

PAUL *points to where he wants him to go.*

PAUL: Sit on the waterfront with me and we'll talk more.

JONATHAN *starts to exit.*

PAUL: Jonathan...JONATHAN....

Runs to JONATHAN *to stop him from leaving.*

PAUL: DO IT!!!!

JONATHAN: Paul, these people have to go home. They have other things in their lives to do. And so do you.

PAUL: No I don't. I can't. I've tried. Last week, I really was downtown. And I went to that stupid bar. I shouldn't have been there. I felt like I was cheating on you. People stared at me. I felt so alone.

And this guy came up to me. And he was...he was...really

nice. He asked me if I wanted to dance. I said no and left. It scared me to death to think about dancing with him. To even be talking to him. I was betraying you. Turning my back on you. So I left. And I did go down to the waterfront. I remember the water really did look like it was steaming. The fog was lingering just above. And it looked so inviting. Hypnotizing. A way to escape...from everything.

JONATHAN: You may not have jumped into the harbour, but you have stopped living. You'd rather have a relationship with a memory than risk feeling anything in the present. And you've invited everyone here in this room to watch it.

PAUL: I just wanted to show everyone. Show everyone how great you are. And it makes me feel closer to you. What's wrong with that?

JONATHAN: Nothing. Oh Boo, nothing. It's wonderful. It's beautiful. But it's not real. It's time for our ending.

PAUL: I can't.

JONATHAN: Why?

PAUL: Because...because *(he whispers)* I don't have an ending.

They both laugh sadly.

PAUL: The way you left. It's not right. There's so much I still wanted to say. So much I need to know. Did I let you down? Did you suffer? Everyone says no. But...but I need... I need *YOU* to tell me.

JONATHAN: I can't give you that. You know the reality. I can't answer you.

PAUL *hangs his head, defeated. Pause.*

JONATHAN: Do you think I suffered?

PAUL: I like...I like to think you didn't know. That you had no idea what happened. A quick flash, like when the lights go out. The doctor said it would have happened "instantaneously." That you wouldn't have known. I like to believe that. She also said it didn't matter how I did the chest compressions. Blood wasn't getting to your heart. I tried so hard to save you. All that pumping. And it wasn't even making a difference.

JONATHAN: See. When you listen, really listen, you find the answers you need.

PAUL: Except for *YOU*. I can't listen to *YOU*.

JONATHAN: If I was here, what would I say about that night?

PAUL: I think...I think if you were here you'd say—

JONATHAN: I am so proud of you. How brave you were. I know how much you tried. You did not let me down.

PAUL: And I think if I told you I felt guilty every time I enjoyed...anything, you'd probably say something very matter of fact like—

JONATHAN: Go ahead, live it up. Sure, I don't know what you're doing. I'm dead!

PAUL: And then you'd probably say—

JONATHAN: But if you really wanna make me happy, go get a haircut.

PAUL: Happy. I remember that. You always used to say when we were talking about jobs, where to live, taking on writing projects—

JONATHAN: Whatever makes you happy will make me happy.

PAUL: And if I told you I felt like I was betraying you every time I even thought about accepting an invitation from someone else—

CARL *enters.*

JONATHAN: The only way you can betray me is not giving your heart what it needs.

CARL: Hey, how's it going?

PAUL: And, if I asked you if it was okay...if maybe...it was okay with you—

JONATHAN: I don't want you to live in the past. Don't let the memory of me cripple you.

CARL: I don't know if you remember me from the other night? Downtown at the bar?

JONATHAN: Tell me what you see, Paul.

PAUL *looks around.*

PAUL: A theatre...lights...people.

JONATHAN: What else?

PAUL *looks at* CARL.

PAUL: A chance?

CARL: We chatted for a few minutes.

JONATHAN: I think it's time for your ending, Boo.

CARL: Well I guess I did most of the chatting.

PAUL: *(to* JONATHAN*)* I will always, always—

JONATHAN: I know. This thou perceivest, which makes thy love more strong...

PAUL: To love that well which thou must leave ere long.

JONATHAN *slowly steps away from* PAUL, *as if to exit. He stops, turns, and waits.*

PAUL: Jonathan...exits stage right.

JONATHAN *slowly exits as* PAUL *watches.*

Lights change back to show lighting.

CARL: Well, you seem like you're kinda busy so maybe I'll see you later.

PAUL: I do remember you. I kinda took off in a hurry. I'm sorry.

CARL: That's okay. I've run out of that bar lots of times too. The place can get to you. Well, I hope things are better.

PAUL: Um...yeah...I think...they're starting to get better.

CARL: Well, good. I was just heading for a coffee. Maybe I could buy you one?

PAUL: Yeah.... Yeah...sure...that would be nice.

CARL: Yeah? Are you ready to go now?

Pause. PAUL *looks at the water and then back at* CARL.

PAUL: Yes. I'm ready.

PAUL *and* CARL *exit. Lights fade.*

END OF PLAY

PAUL DAVID POWER's work includes roles in over thirty stage plays across the country, as well as directing and producing. He was President of the Liffey Players Drama Society in Calgary, Alberta, for three years, Artistic Director for Hubcity Theatre in Moncton, New Brunswick, for five years, and Artistic Associate for the Shakespeare by the Sea Festival in St. John's, Newfoundland, for three years.

Paul identifies as a disabled artist. He owns Power Productions, a professional theatre company dedicated to the development of works and artists with a focus on the disabled, Deaf, and MAD Arts domain.

He lives in St. John's.